For the Teacher

This reproducible study guide to use in conjunction with a specifc novel consists of lessons for guided reading. Written in chapter-by-chapter format, the guide contains a synopsis, pre-reading activities, vocabulary and comprehension exercises, as well as extension activities to be used as follow-up to the novel.

NOVEL-TIES are either for whole class instruction using a single title or for group instruction where each group uses a different novel appropriate to its reading level. Depending upon the amount of time allotted to it in the classroom, each novel, with its guide and accompanying lessons, may be completed in two to four weeks.

The first step in using NOVEL-TIES is to distribute to each student a copy of the novel and a folder containing all of the duplicated worksheets. Begin instruction by selecting several pre-reading activities in order to set the stage for the reading ahead. Vocabulary exercises for each chapter always precede the reading so that new words will be reinforced in the context of the book. Use the questions on the chapter worksheets for class discussion or as written exercises.

The benefits of using NOVEL-TIES are numerous. Students read good literature in the original, rather than in abridged or edited form. The good reading habits, formed by practice in focusing on interpretive comprehension and literary techniques, will be transferred to the books students read independently. Passive readers become active, avid readers.

Novel-Ties® are printed on recycled paper.

SYNOPSIS

Phillip Enright lives on the picturesque island of Curaçao whose peacefulness is shattered by the outbreak of World War II. Phillip's mother is determined to take Phillip home to Virginia, where she feels they will be safe. She is also eager to leave Curaçao because of her prejudice against the native-born West Indian population.

The ship that is carrying Phillip and his mother to the United States is torpedoed by a German submarine while they are at sea. In the confusion that follows, Phillip becomes separated from his mother. He is left afloat at sea on a raft. His only companion is an elderly black man named Timothy.

At first, Phillip barely tolerates Timothy, but he soon begins to depend more and more on Timothy's wisdom and gentleness to survive their ordeal. This dependence increases dramatically when Phillip loses his eyesight, a delayed result of the head injury he suffered during the shipwreck. Timothy gradually becomes Phillip's trusted mentor as they leave their raft and settle on a small, deserted cay in the Caribbean. Although Timothy has no formal education, his practical knowledge helps Phillip cope with his disability and develop some independence. When Timothy dies during a raging storm on the island, Phillip's skills are put to the test.

Alone, except for a cat who also survived the shipwreck, Phillip remembers Timothy's wisdom and keeps himself alive until he is spotted by a boat and finally rescued. Phillip arrives home, and although his eyesight is restored through surgery, he is forever changed by his ordeal. He hopes one day to set sail again, find his island, and honor the memory of Timothy whose courage and love gave him the strength to survive.

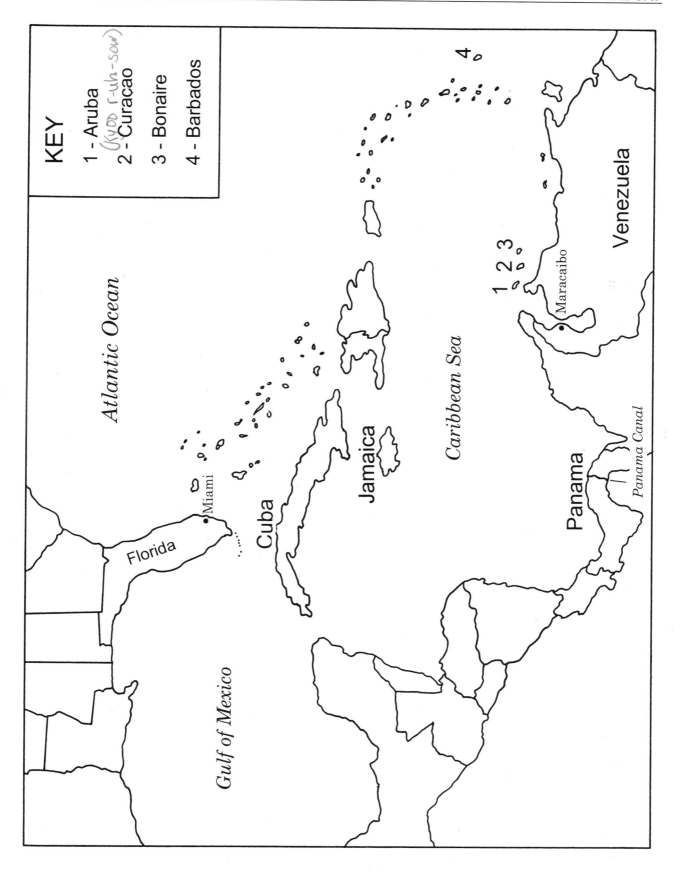

KEY
1 - Aruba (uh r-uh-sow)
2 - Curacao
3 - Bonaire
4 - Barbados

Atlantic Ocean

4

Venezuela

Maracaibo

1 2 3

Caribbean Sea

Jamaica

Cuba

Miami

Florida

Panama

Panama Canal

Gulf of Mexico

ANTICIPATION GUIDE

The theme of a book expresses a general truth about life or human beings. In this novel, the author conveys his feelings about prejudice, which exists when a person is judged solely according to race, religion, gender, sexual orientation, or nationality.

Below are ten statements that deal with prejudice. Before you read *The Cay*, tell whether you agree or disagree with each statement by marking a *Yes* or *No* next to each statement under the column "YOU." After you read *The Cay*, tell whether the author agrees with each of the statements by marking *Yes* or *No* in the "AUTHOR" column.

	YOU	AUTHOR
1. Always judge people based on first impressions.		
2. People who belong to the same ethnic or religious group are alike in most ways.		
3. Prejudice hurts only its victims.		
4. Prejudice hurts the aggressor as well as the victim.		
5. Children adopt the prejudices of their parents.		
6. Prejudice is learned.		
7. Prejudice reduction can be taught.		
8. Only experience can change attitudes of prejudice.		
9. Strong feelings of prejudice will never change.		
10. Problems of prejudice have been solved in society today.		

PRE-READING ACTIVITIES

1. Preview the book by reading the title and the author's name and by looking at the illustration on the cover. What do you think the book will be about? Where and when does it take place? Have you read any other books by the same author?

2. Look up the word "stereotype" in a dictionary. Then discuss with your classmates the impact of stereotyping on ethnic and racial groups in our society today. What examples of stereotyping exist on television, in newspapers, and in magazines? What are the negative effects of stereotyping upon the victims as well as upon the perpetrators?

3. **Cooperative Learning Activity:** With a group of your classmates, discuss how prejudice and stereotyping may be present in your community. Find examples of stereotyping in the media. Together with the other members of your group, devise a plan to reduce prejudice and eliminate the practice of stereotyping.

4. Claiming that something will happen often causes it to occur. This is called a self-fulfilling prophecy. How might the victims of prejudice and stereotyping become products of self-fulfilling prophecies at school and work?

5. This novel is dedicated to Dr. Martin Luther King, Jr. and his dream of a society without prejudice. Read Dr. King's famous "I've Got a Dream" speech and predict how its theme might be woven into the fabric of the novel.

6. *The Cay* was published in 1968, the year that Dr. Martin Luther King, Jr. was assassinated. Do some research to learn about the state of civil rights for minorities at that time. Read about some of the major events such as the Supreme Court rulings that put an end to segregation in public schools, the senseless killings at Kent State University, and the Montgomery bus boycott.

7. What are some of the lasting effects of the civil rights struggle that took place during the years from 1954 to 1968? How have some of the changes been eroded? What kinds of reform are still necessary?

8. Look up the word "cay" in a dictionary. Then discuss with your classmates the elements of survival on a deserted island. Be sure to discuss shelters that could be built, food to be foraged, and clothing that might be needed.

9. Look at the map on page four of this study guide to acquaint yourself with the geographical area featured in this book. Look at it again while you read in order to understand the events as they occur.

10. Locate a travel poster or tourist brochure showing the harbor of Curaçao. [kyoo r-uh-sow] Find out why the houses are typical of those found in Holland.

11. Do some research and consult the map on page four of this study guide to find out why the Germans in World War II were interested in the oil that was drilled in Venezuela and refined on the Dutch islands of Aruba and Curaçao.

12. **Science Connection:** Do some research to learn about undersea coral formations and coral reefs. Learn how they provide protection and spawning ground for many sea creatures, but may cause problems for ships. Find out why coral reefs are in danger and how conservationists are trying to protect them.

CHAPTERS 1, 2

Vocabulary: The following words have a general definition as well as a nautical definition. Use a dictionary to help you fill in the chart below.

	General Definition	Nautical Definition
1. bow		forward part of ship
2. stern		back part of ship
3. tug		boat that pulls others
4. deck		
5. pitch		Imaginary line running through horizontal axis

Additional Seafaring Words: Use a dictionary to find the meanings of each of these nautical words:

1. schooner _____

2. trade winds _____

3. starboard _____

4. leeward _____

5. ballast _____

Questions:

1. Why did Phillip and the people of Curaçao fear for their own safety even though the major events of World War II were taking place in Europe and the South Pacific?
2. Why were the islands of Aruba and Curaçao in potential danger of German attack?
3. On the day of the U-boat sighting, what actions revealed that Phillip was not as worried about his safety as his mother was?
4. How did Phillip's parents disagree about living in Curaçao?
5. Why did Mrs. Enright decide to leave Curaçao with Phillip? Do you think that they really had to leave, or that she was looking for an excuse to leave?
6. Why didn't Phillip want to leave Curaçao?

Chapters 1, 2 (cont.)

Questions for Discussion:

1. Do you think Phillip's father should have insisted that his family remain in Curaçao?
2. Do you think that Phillip shared his mother's prejudice against black people?
3. What kind of event might motivate you to want to leave your home?

Literary Devices:

I. *Point of View* — Point of view in literature refers to the voice telling the story. It could be the narrator or one of the characters in the story. Who is telling this story?

_____

Why do you think the author has chosen this point of view?

_____

II. *Simile* — A simile is a figure of speech in which two unlike objects are compared using the words "like" or "as." For example:

> Like silent, hungry sharks that swim in the darkness of the sea, the German submarines arrived in the middle of the night.

What is being compared?

_____

What is the effect of this comparison?

_____

Writing Activity:

In the opening pages of the novel, the author provides important background information. Fill in the chart below with information found in these chapters. Then use this information as notes to write a newspaper article about the events that led to Mrs. Enright's decision to leave Curaçao.

WHO (is the story about)?	
WHAT (has happened)?	
WHERE (does the story take place)?	
WHEN (does the story take place)?	
WHY (is this happening)?	

CHAPTERS 3, 4

Vocabulary: Draw a line from each word on the left to its definition on the right. Then use the numbered words to fill in the blanks in the sentences below.

1. deftly
2. rippled
3. blurt
4. hazy
5. flimsy
6. drill
7. plunge

a. utter suddenly
b. any strict, repetitive training or instruction
c. misty
d. skillfully
e. fall rapidly or forcefully
f. weak; unstable
g. characterized by small waves

. . . .

1. The water _____ in each spot where a pebble landed in the pond.

2. The surgeon _____ stitched the open wound.

3. The suitcase was made of such _____ material that it tore the first time we used it.

4. It was refreshing to _____ into the cool water on a hot summer day.

5. It was too _____ to see whether the golf ball landed on the green.

6. The officer knew he had to conduct a _____ before his men would be ready to load a rifle on the battlefield.

7. The children were so excited about the surprise party that they were afraid they would _____ out the secret.

Questions:

1. How did Phillip and his mother become separated?
2. What were Phillip's first reactions when he discovered he had been shipwrecked on a raft with a black man?
3. Why did Phillip have negative feelings toward Timothy even though he was trying to be helpful and offer consolation?
4. How did Timothy comfort Phillip when he displayed terror over his blindness? What did Timothy's words tell about his ability to sympathize with Phillip's fear?

Chapters 3, 4 (cont.)

Questions for Discussion:

1. Although Phillip has been taught to call adults, "mister," he called the black man "Timothy." Timothy, on the other hand, addressed Phillip as "young bahss." What did this reveal about the relationship between the two and the relationship between the two ethnic groups on the island of Curaçao?

2. Why do you think Phillip directed his anger toward his mother and Timothy?

Science Connection:

Do some research to learn about the causes and effects of a brain concussion. Find out about the best first aid and long-range treatment for a concussion.

Writing Activity:

Since this story is told from Phillip's point of view, Timothy's feelings about the shipwreck and his feelings about Phillip are not described. Based upon what you know about Timothy, write about the same set of events from Timothy's point of view. Do not attempt to imitate Timothy's dialect.

CHAPTERS 5, 6

Vocabulary: Synonyms are words with similar meanings. Draw a line from each word in column A to its synonym in column B. Then use the words in column A to fill in the blanks in the sentences below.

	A		B
1.	douse	a.	searched
2.	gasp	b.	nervous
3.	scanned	c.	gulp
4.	faint	d.	serene
5.	anxious	e.	soak
6.	calm	f.	dim

. . . .

1. I began to _____ for air as the room filled with smoke.

2. The painted lines on the road grew _____ after so many years of heavy traffic.

3. Afraid that I was unprepared, I became _____ on the day of the test.

4. Before you leave for vacation, you should _____ the plants in your house with water.

5. If you have little children at home, it is better to choose a(n) _____ puppy instead of a frisky one.

6. I _____ the distant road, hoping I would see you returning home.

Questions:

1. Why did Timothy burn cloth to make a torch?

2. Why did Timothy warn Phillip not to put his hands into the water?

Chapters 5, 6 (cont.)

3. In what ways was Timothy becoming Phillip's eyes?

4. Why did Timothy become angry with Phillip?

5. How did Phillip and Timothy disagree over the island?

Questions for Discussion:

1. Do you think Timothy really believed that he and Phillip would be discovered by a plane or a ship?

2. Why do you think there were not many search vessels in the water or flying overhead?

3. Do you think Timothy's rage was justified when Phillip fell overboard?

4. Do you think Timothy and Phillip would have a better chance to be rescued from the raft or from the island?

Science Connection:

Do some research to learn about sharks and about the bird with the strange name—the booby. Learn about their habits and where they can be found. Find pictures of these creatures and put them on a classroom bulletin board.

Writing Activities:

1. Pretend you are Phillip's father and have received news of the shipwreck. You are willing to give a reward to anyone who finds your son. Write an advertisement for a newspaper asking for help and giving the information needed to carry out the rescue.

2. Imagine that you are a radio or television newscaster. Write a news broadcast describing the events that led up to the shipwreck. Be sure to use dramatic prose. You may tape record or videotape your broadcast. If you are videotaping, you might use a large map to point out the location of the event.

Chapters 5, 6 (cont.)

Literary Element: Characterization

One person can have many different and sometimes contradictory personality traits. In the chart below tell how Timothy exhibited each of these traits:

TIMOTHY

Trait	Example
kindness	
tenderness	
sympathy	
strength	
stubborness	
bad temper	

CHAPTERS 7, 8

Vocabulary: Use the context to figure out the meaning of the underlined word in each of the following sentences. Compare your definition with a dictionary definition.

1. Even the captain became <u>alarmed</u> when the ship began to fill with water.

    Your definition   _____

    Dictionary definition _____

2. We listened to the <u>surf</u> pound against the shore as we waited for the storm to hit.

    Your definition   _____

    Dictionary definition _____

3. After studying for weeks, my sister was <u>confident</u> that she would win the spelling bee.

    Your definition   _____

    Dictionary definition _____

4. Looking <u>gravely</u> at the accused man, the judge pronounced him guilty.

    Your definition   _____

    Dictionary definition _____

5. Once fog settled on the bay, <u>navigation</u> of our sailboat became impossible.

    Your definition   _____

    Dictionary definition _____

6. Smoke from the <u>smoldering</u> campfires made our eyes tear.

    Your definition   _____

    Dictionary definition _____

Questions:

1. Phillip felt dependent upon Timothy at the same time as he felt superior to him. What two events revealed Phillip's conflicting feelings?
2. Why did Timothy think it would be unlikely for Phillip and him to be rescued?

Chapters 7, 8 (cont.)

3. Why couldn't Timothy permit Phillip to join him when he explored the reef?

4. Why was Phillip able to remain hopeful despite the tragedy of his present condition?

5. What did Timothy do shortly after their arrival on the cay to provide them with shelter and food?

6. How did Phillip learn that Timothy could not spell? What did this reveal about Timothy's education and the kind of education the black population received in Curaçao?

Questions for Discussion:

1. Why do you think Phillip harbored feelings of resentment toward Timothy?

2. Do you think Timothy should have told Phillip about the unlikelihood of being rescued?

3. How long do you think Phillip and Timothy could survive on the island? What would they have to do to stay alive and healthy?

4. How might Phillip's feelings about living on the island and his relationship with Timothy have been different if he were not blind?

Art Connection:

Use the descriptions found in Chapters Seven and Eight to draw a picture of the cay where Timothy and Phillip were marooned. Include a sketch of the hut that Timothy built.

Science Connection:

Do some research to find out about edible sea life in the waters of the Caribbean. Learn whether the sea life is plentiful and how it is caught.

Chapters 7, 8 (cont.)

Literary Element: Conflict

Conflict, or the clash of opposing forces, takes many forms in literature and often provides the excitement in a story. In the chart below tell how each kind of conflict is revealed in *The Cay*.

Person *vs.* Person ——

Person *vs.* Nature ——

Person *vs.* Self ——

Writing Activities:

1. Write about how these three kinds of conflicts have existed in your life. Tell whether the conflicts have been resolved.
2. Write about a time when you were dependent upon another person. Describe the situation and convey your feelings about this dependency.

CHAPTERS 9 - 11

Vocabulary: Draw a line from each word on the left to its definition on the right. Then use the numbered words to fill in the blanks in the sentences below.

1.	stun	a.	save from being destroyed
2.	burst	b.	taught; instructed
3.	submerge	c.	shock; surprise
4.	stranded	d.	put under water
5.	salvage	e.	torn or ragged
6.	tutored	f.	explode; blow up
7.	tattered	g.	deserted; helpless

· ·

1. After the fire, I tried to _____ my photographs from the burnt wreckage.

2. I was _____ at home after I broke my leg and was unable to attend school.

3. We saw the firecracker _____ in the air, sending tails of light into the sky.

4. How would you obtain food if you were _____ on a desert island?

5. After our hiking trip, I discarded my dirty, _____ clothing.

6. His sudden appearance after a three-year absence will _____ his family.

7. On a hot summer day, it is a relief to _____ your entire body in the swimming pool.

Questions:

1. What event signaled a complete change in Timothy and Phillip's relationship?
2. Why did Timothy weave vines into a rope for Phillip?
3. Why were Phillip and Timothy happy when it rained hard?
4. How did Timothy keep Phillip from feeling sorry for himself?
5. How did Timothy attempt to improve their luck?

Questions for Discussion:

1. Why do you think Timothy was trying to make Phillip more independent?
2. Why do you think that Phillip's attitude toward Timothy changed?

Chapters 9 - 11 (cont.)

3. Do you think that Timothy was being too hard on Phillip, or that his training and discipline were necessary? Do you think Timothy should have expressed more sympathy for Phillip?

4. Do you think there is any relationship between the carved cat and evil spirits? Do you have any superstitious beliefs? What might you do to have good luck or prevent bad luck?

Literary Devices:

I. *Simile* — What is being compared in the following simile:

The rain sounded like bullets hitting on the dried palm frond roof.

_____

Why is this an apt comparison?

_____

_____

II. *Irony* — Irony refers to an unusual twist of fate. Why is it ironic that Phillip, who has come from a background of prejudice, has been marooned on an island with a black man and has become blinded?

_____

_____

Prediction:

Phillip says that their luck doesn't change. It gets worse. What additional hardships do you think they might face?

_____

_____

_____

_____

Writing Activity:

Imagine that Phillip is able to record his early impressions of the cay and his feelings about Timothy on a tape recorder. Write a short narrative that might express Phillip's thoughts after a week on the cay.

CHAPTERS 12, 13

Vocabulary: Antonyms are words with opposite meanings. Draw a line from each word in column A to its antonym in column B. Then use the words in column A to fill in the blanks in the sentences below.

	A		B
1.	harsh	a.	death
2.	squatting	b.	standing
3.	jagged	c.	boulder
4.	survival	d.	flexible
5.	rigid	e.	shout
6.	mumble	f.	gentle
7.	pebble	g.	mound
8.	crevice	h.	smooth

. . . .

1. As we hiked up the mountain, we were careful not to let our feet slip into the _____.

2. If you _____ into the telephone answering machine, I will not get your message.

3. I cut my ankle as I tripped on the _____ rock.

4. The children were _____ around the campfire, trying to get warm.

5. Once the soft plaster dried on the wall, it became _____.

6. Unprepared for the _____ northern winter, I packed only warm-weather clothing.

7. _____ in the wild depends on using the natural surroundings to create a shelter and find food.

8. Just a little _____ inside my shoe made walking extremely uncomfortable.

Questions:

1. Why could Timothy's malaria only be treated with cool water?
2. How did Phillip show his growing self-sufficiency during Timothy's bout with malaria?
3. What lasting result did the latest bout of malaria have on Timothy?

Chapters 12, 13 (cont.)

4. Why did Timothy want Phillip to be able to fish on his own?
5. Why did Phillip climb the coconut palm despite his fear?

Questions for Discussion:

1. What do you think Phillip really meant when he asked Timothy, "Are you still black"?
2. How did Phillip's blindness make it easier for him to become close to Timothy and cast aside his former prejudice? How had Phillip's prejudice caused him to misjudge Timothy's character?

Literary Device: Symbolism

A symbol in literature is an object, an act, or a person that represents an idea or a set of ideas. Consider the act of Phillip's climbing the coconut tree. How was this a symbolic act? What was its significance?

_____

_____

_____

Literary Element: Characterization

Use a Venn diagram such as the one below to compare Phillip when he first came to the island and now after spending time on the island. Use the overlapping part of the circles to record those aspects of his character that have not changed.

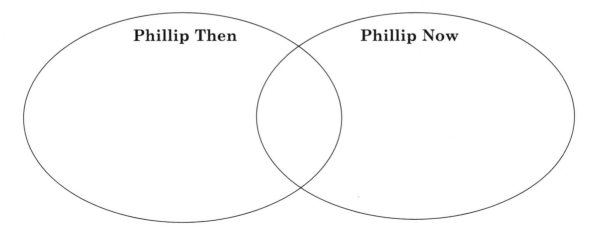

Phillip Then   Phillip Now

Writing Activity:

Imagine you are Phillip. Write a letter to your parents in which you tell them all about Timothy.

CHAPTERS 14, 15

Vocabulary: Replace each underlined word in the sentences below with its synonym from the Word Box. Write the word you choose on the line below the sentence.

```
              WORD BOX
    eerie       erect       limp
    massive     sparingly   violence
```

1. The <u>huge</u> building blocked our view of the park.

    _____

2. He felt exhausted and <u>weak</u> after he ran the race.

    _____

3. If you want to measure your height, you must stand <u>upright</u>.

    _____

4. You should spend your money <u>economically</u> if you want it to last until you get your next allowance.

    _____

5. Their little hut could not protect them from the <u>rage</u> of the storm.

    _____

6. Before the storm hit, the sky had a <u>strange</u> yellow glow.

    _____

Questions:

1. How did Timothy know that a storm was coming? What did he do to prepare for the storm?

2. Why did Timothy call the approaching storm a "freak"?

3. Why was Phillip afraid of surviving the storm alone?

4. What sacrifice did Timothy make on Phillip's behalf during the hurricane?

Chapters 14, 15 (cont.)

Questions for Discussion:

1. Upon realizing that Timothy had died, what do you think Phillip meant when he said, "There are times when you are beyond tears"?
2. If Phillip's mother were aware of Timothy's sacrifice on her son's behalf do you think her views about black people would change?

Science Activity:

Do some research to learn about hurricanes. Find out how a hurricane forms, the nature of the storm, and the kind of damage it may cause. Then evaluate whether the description of the hurricane in *The Cay* is correct, according to your research.

Writing Activities:

1. The author has carefully described the arrival of a hurricane on the cay. Imagine that you are a meteorologist (weather forecaster) and write a television report of this occurrence. Write a brief narrative describing the onset of the storm, the actual event, its effect on the cay, and its aftermath.
2. Imagine you are Phillip and write a journal entry describing your thoughts and feelings on the day of the storm.

CHAPTERS 16 - 19

Vocabulary: Draw a line from each word on the left to its definition on the right. Then use the numbered words to fill in the blanks in the sentences below.

1. grope
2. legacy
3. yank
4. precise
5. debris
6. earnest

a. exact; accurate
b. serious
c. pull or jerk
d. inheritance
e. rubbish; remains of anything destroyed
f. search in the dark by feeling

. . . .

1. During the power blackout, we had to _____ in the drawer for the flashlight.

2. There will be less pain if I _____ the bandage off quickly.

3. With a(n) _____ expression on his face, the coach reviewed the rules of the game.

4. Every answer in a mathematics exam must be _____.

5. After the storm, the beach was littered with _____.

6. My family was so poor that my only _____ was their musical talent.

Language Study: Onomatopoeia

Onomatopoeia is a term used when a word copies the sound of the object it names. Below are examples of onomatopoeia found in these chapters. Tell what objects might make these sounds.

1. rustle   _____
2. crackle   _____
3. sizzle   _____
4. sloshing _____

What other words do you know that are examples of onomatopoeia? Tell what objects might make these sounds.

_____
_____
_____
_____

Chapters 16 - 19 (cont.)

Questions:

1. What immediate task faced Phillip at the end of the storm?
2. What was Timothy's legacy to Phillip, and how did it help him continue to fight for his survival?
3. Why did Phillip use sea grape to make a fire?
4. Why was Phillip more depressed after the plane passed the island than at any other time during his ordeal?
5. What was the one object Phillip took with him from the island? What was its special significance to him?
6. How much time had passed between Phillip's arrival on the cay and his rescue?
7. What was Phillip's dream for the future?

Questions for Discussion:

1. How do you think Phillip's blindness protected him from fear after Timothy's death?
2. Why do you think the adult rescuers did not believe Phillip's story at first?
3. Why do you think Phillip's mother apologized to Phillip when they were reunited?

Science Connection:

Do some research to learn about the moray eel. From your study, do you think that the creature that stung Phillip was a moray eel? Find a picture of this creature and place it on a classroom bulletin board.

Writing Activity:

Imagine you are a reporter assigned to write an article about Phillip's rescue. Prepare an article for a newspaper, including the important information of *who, what, where, when*, and *why*.

CLOZE ACTIVITY

The following passage has been taken from Chapter Eleven of the book. Read it through completely and then go back and fill in each blank with a word that makes sense. When you have finished you may compare your language with that of the author.

Slowly, I was beginning to know the island. By myself, keeping my

_____¹ in the damp sand, which meant I _____² near the water,

I walked the whole _____³ around it. Timothy was very proud of

_____.⁴

From walking over it, feeling it, and _____⁵ to it, I think I knew

what _____⁶ cay looked like. As Timothy said, it _____⁷

shaped like a melon, or a turtle, _____⁸ up from the sea to our ridge

_____⁹ the palms flapped all day and night _____¹⁰ the light

trade wind.

The beach, I _____¹¹ believed, was about forty yards wide in

_____¹² places, stretching all the way around the _____.¹³ On

one end, to the east, was _____¹⁴ low coral reef that extended several

hundred yards, awash in many places.

I know it _____¹⁵ to the east because one morning _____¹⁶

was down there with Timothy when the _____¹⁷ came up, and I could feel

the _____¹⁸ on my face from that direction.

The sea grape, a few _____¹⁹ tall at the edge of the beach,

_____²⁰ higher farther back, grew along the slopes _____²¹ the

hill on all sides. There was also some other brush that did not feel like sea grape,

but Timothy did not know the name of it.

POST-READING ACTIVITIES AND QUESTIONS

1. Return to the Anticipation Guide on page three of this study guide and fill in the column marked "AUTHOR." Based upon the implied opinions of the author, do you think he would have agreed or disagreed with each of the statements? Now that you have completed the novel, are there any opinions that you would like to change in the "YOU" column?

2. In what way is this book a memorial to Dr. Martin Luther King, Jr. and to his dreams, as stated in the dedication at the beginning of the book?

3. When Phillip returned home, he was a changed person. Can you think of an experience of your own that left a lasting impression on you and changed you in some way?

4. Discuss "stereotyping" in the light of the events that occurred in this novel. How had Phillip's initial reaction to Timothy been molded by the stereotypes of blacks that he had learned from society? Do you think it takes a dramatic event or a crisis to undermine the stereotypes and prejudices that are part of our lives? Or do you think it is possible for change to come about in other ways?

5. Based upon Phillip's experience on the cay and any other knowledge you may possess, write a short survival manual for a person who may become marooned on a tropical cay. Be sure to provide information concerning the basic elements of survival: food, shelter, and clothing.

6. Imagine you are Phillip and you are being interviewed on a television talk show after you have returned home. With another classmate playing the role of host, present this interview to your class.

7. **Science Connection:** Place the following species mentioned in the book into appropriate categories. Find pictures to illustrate any of the species. Compare the categories you created with those of your classmates.

bamboo	conch	mussel	sea urchin
banana	flying fish	palm	shark
barracuda	honeysuckle	papaya	skate
booby	langosta	pompano	turtle
calico scallop	lizard	scorpion	
coconut	moray eel	sea grape	

SUGGESTIONS FOR FURTHER READING

*   Cleaver, Bill, and Vera Cleaver. *Where the Lilies Bloom.* New American Library.

    Defoe, Daniel. *Robinson Crusoe.* New American Library.

    Eckert, Allen. *Incident at Hawk's Hill.* Random House.

*   George, Jean C. *Julie of the Wolves.* HarperCollins.

*   _____. *My Side of the Mountain.* Penguin.

    _____. *River Rats.* Scholastic.

*   Holman, Felice. *Slake's Limbo.* Simon & Schuster.

*   Konigsburg, E.L. *From the Mixed-Up Files of Mrs. Basil E. Frankweiler.*
          Random House.

    Mathieson, David. *Trial By Wilderness.* Houghton Mifflin.

    Mazer, Harry. *The Island Keeper.* Random House.

*   O'Dell, Scott. *The Island of the Blue Dolphins.* Random House.

*   Paulsen, Gary. *Hatchet.* Penguin.

    Read, Piers P. *Alive: The Story of the Andes Survivors.* HarperCollins.

    Roth, Arthur. *Iceberg Hermit.* Scholastic.

*   Sperry, Armstrong. *Call it Courage.* Simon & Schuster.

Some Other Books by Theodore Taylor

*   *The Bomb.* HarperCollins.

*   *The Maldonado Miracle.* HarperCollins.

    The Odyssey of Ben O'Neal. HarperCollins.

    Rocket Island. HarperCollins.

    Sweet Friday Island. Scholastic.

    Teetoncey. HarperCollins.

*   *Timothy of the Cay.* HarperCollins.

*   *The Trouble with Tuck.* HarperCollins.

    Tuck Triumphant. HarperCollins.

    Walking Up a Rainbow. Random House.

*   NOVEL-TIES Study Guides are available for these titles.

ANSWER KEY

Chapters 1, 2

Vocabulary: 1. bow: GD – bend of the head or knee; ND – forward end of a boat 2. stern: GD – serious; ND – rear of a ship 3. tug: GD – pull forcefully; ND – small ship used for towing large vessels 4. deck: GD – pack of playing cards; ND – any open platform 5. pitch: GD – throw; ND – plunge with alternate rise and fall of bow and stern; 1. schooner – type of sailing vessel having at least a foremast and main mast 2. trade winds – easterly winds that dominate the tropics 3. starboard – toward the right side of a ship 4. leeward – toward the side of the ship from which the wind blows 5. ballast – heavy material used to stabilize a vessel

Questions: 1. People in Curaçao feared for their safety because the Lago Oil Refinery in nearby Aruba was attacked in February 1942, oil tankers were sunk, and a German submarine was sighted in waters near Curaçao. 2. Aruba and Curaçao were in danger of German attack because these islands stored and refined oil, which was needed for the war effort. 3. It was clear that Phillip was more excited than scared on the day of the U-boat sighting because he disobeyed his mother's orders to stay home and went down to play at the fort instead. 4. Mrs. Enright missed the security and safety of Virginia. She missed the change of seasons, she missed her friends, and she hated the constant smell of oil. She did not like to be in a place where there were so many black people. Mr. Enright was happy to be in Curaçao, contributing to the war effort. 5. Mrs. Enright decided to leave Curaçao after the oil tanker the *Empire Tern* was torpedoed and sunk by a German submarine right off the coast. Answers to the second part of the question will vary. 6. Phillip was sad to leave Curaçao because he loved the beauty of the island and knew he would miss his father and his friends.

Chapters 3, 4

Vocabulary: 1. d 2. g 3. a 4. c 5. f 6. b 7. e; 1. rippled 2. deftly 3. flimsy 4. plunge 5. hazy 6. drill 7. blurt

Questions: 1. As Phillip and his mother were being lowered in a lifeboat from the burning ship, the boat loosened and caused them to plunge into the water. When Phillip regained consciousness, he realized he had become separated from his mother during the rescue. 2. When Phillip first realized he was shipwrecked on a raft with a black man, he was terrified by Timothy's size and overall appearance. He also found the man repugnant. 3. Phillip's negative feelings were a reflection of his mother's prejudice toward black people. 4. Timothy tried to be reassuring and convince Phillip that the blindness was just temporary. He displayed warmth and tender sympathy for the boy.

Chapters 5, 6

Vocabulary:
Questions: 1. e 2. c 3. a 4. f 5. b 6. d; 1. gasp 2. faint 3. anxious 4. douse 5. calm 6. scanned
1. When he saw a search plane flying overhead, Timothy burned a piece of cloth to serve as a torch to attract attention. 2. Timothy warned Phillip not to put his hands in the water because it would attract sharks to their raft. 3. Timothy was becoming Phillip's eyes by patiently describing the scene around him and by telling him about the fish and birds that crossed their path. He also warned him of dangers he could not see. 4. Timothy became enraged when Phillip tumbled off the raft, exposing both of them to the danger of sharks. 5. Phillip wanted to stay aboard the raft, thinking they could be better seen by a searching ship or plane. Timothy insisted they would be safer on land.

Chapters 7, 8

Vocabulary: 1. alarmed – frightened 2. surf – swell of the sea that breaks along the shore 3. confident – certain 4. gravely – seriously 5. navigation – act of moving on water 6. smoldering – burning without flame

Questions: 1. Phillip believed Timothy was foolish to debark at this island, but feared being left alone while Timothy explored or went to the reef to catch langosta. Phillip felt superior to Timothy when he realized that Timothy could not spell, but needed Phillip to outline the word "Help" in the sand. 2. Realizing that the island was surrounded by a coral reef that

made navigation near the cay extremely dangerous, Timothy concluded that rescue was unlikely. 3. Timothy explored the reef alone because he wanted to see for himself how dangerous it would be before he risked taking Phillip with him. 4. Phillip remained hopeful because Timothy kept offering him hope of rescue. 5. Shortly after their arrival on the cay, Timothy built a hut and fished for langosta. 6. Phillip learned that Timothy could not spell when Timothy asked Phillip to write the word "Help" in the sand. This suggested that the black population in Curaçao received very little education.

Chapters 9-11

Vocabulary: 1. c 2. f 3. d 4. g 5. a 6. b 7. e; 1. salvage 2. tutored 3. burst 4. stranded 5. tattered 6. stun 7. submerge

Questions: 1. After Timothy slapped Phillip for calling him a stupid black man, Phillip was stunned into realizing that Timothy was a valuable friend. 2. Timothy created a rope so that it could guide Phillip down to the beach or let him touch off the fire if a rescue boat seemed near. 3. Timothy and Phillip were pleased with the hard rain because water collected in the keg that Timothy fashioned and it was refreshing after days of dry heat. 4. Whenever Phillip showed signs of feeling sorry for himself, Timothy would change the subject of their discussion, offer him words of hope, and give him tasks to do. 5. Based on his voodoo belief system, Timothy thought the cat had caused them bad luck. He put Stew Cat in the raft while he carved a wooden cat and nailed it to the roof of the hut to ward off evil spirits.

Chapters 12, 13

Vocabulary: 1. f 2. b 3. h 4. a 5. d 6. e 7. c 8. g; 1. crevice 2. mumble 3. jagged 4. squatting 5. rigid 6. harsh 7. survival 8. pebble

Questions: 1. Without medicine, or even aspirin, on the island, cool water was the only thing available to bring down Timothy's fever. 2. During Timothy's bout with malaria, Phillip dragged him out of the water and sheltered his body from the sun with branches of sea grape. 3. Timothy never totally regained his strength after the latest bout of malaria. 4. Afraid that the next bout of malaria could take his life, Timothy wanted Phillip to be able to fish on his own, which would provide him with the food he needed to survive. 5. Not wanting to disappoint Timothy, who was eager to have fresh coconut, Phillip overcame his fear and climbed the palm.

Chapters 14, 15

Vocabulary: 1. massive 2. limp 3. erect 4. sparingly 5. violence 6. eerie

Questions: 1. Timothy knew that the sound of a shot was really the crash of a wave, signaling the approach of a terrible storm. The stillness of the air and the yellow sky also foretold the storm. Timothy lashed the water keg high on a palm tree; then he tied rope around a sturdy palm to which they might tie their arms during the height of the storm. 2. Timothy called the approaching storm a "freak" because hurricanes usually form in September, not July. 3. Phillip feared the loneliness and he worried about his ability to survive alone. 4. Timothy placed his own body between that of Phillip and the storm. He received the direct lashing of the wind and rain.

Chapters 16-19

Vocabulary: 1. f 2. d 3. c 4. a 5. e 6. b; 1. grope 2. yank 3. earnest 4. precise 5. debris 6. inheritance

Questions: 1. At the end of the storm, Phillip's most immediate task was to bury Timothy. 2. As a legacy, Timothy had left Phillip the water keg, the tin box with matches, and more than a dozen fishing poles. These would enable Phillip to have warmth, signal an approaching ship, and catch fish for food from the waters. 3. Phillip used sea grape because it would make a good signal fire: it had oil in its branches which would create black smoke. 4. Philip's hopes were dashed when the plane passed the island. He now believed that he would never be found and that he would not be able to survive alone. 5. The one item Phillip took with him from the island was Timothy's knife. It probably symbolized all that Timothy had meant to him and his extraordinary wisdom and strength. 6. Four and a half months had passed between Phillip's arrival on the cay and his rescue. 7. Phillip dreamed of returning to the island someday and visiting Timothy's grave.